W. H. AUDEN Poems selected by JOHN FULLER

W. H. AUDEN
Poems selected by JOHN FULLER

faber and faber

First published in 2000
by Faber and Faber Limited
3 Queen Square London WC1N 3AU

Photoset by Parker Typesetting Service, Leicester
Printed in Italy

This selection and introduction © John Fuller, 2000
Poems copyright © 1977, 1991, the Estate of W. H. Auden

John Fuller is hereby identified as editor of
this work in accordance with Section 77
of the Copyright, Designs and Patents Act 1988

A CIP record for this book
is available from the British Library

ISBN 0–571–20348–5

10 9 8 7 6 5 4 3 2

Contents

Textual Note

Early texts of poems from the 1930s have been preferred, but with the titles given to them in Auden's most recent collected editions. All poems and extracts may be found in either *The English Auden* or *Collected Poems*, with the exception of 'Getting Dressed' (my title for the extract from 'In the year of my youth . . .', published in *The Review of English Studies*, ns. vol. xxix, no. 115, August 1978).

Introduction

Auden's range was astonishing. He wrote poems of all kinds, from couplet squibs to book-length 'abstract drama', from advertising songs to oratorios, from film commentary to formal elegy, from comic verse letter to dream allegory, from limericks to libretti, from *vers d'occasion* to political satire. He remoulded the ode, the sonnet-sequence, the dramatic chorus and the prose poem for his age, and more or less invented the mode we tend to call the 'paysage moralisé'. To offer a faithful representation of his work in fewer than a hundred pages is clearly impossible. It would be like representing the art of a three-star Michelin chef (who had mastered the *haute cuisine* of several continents, remembered the regional cooking of his childhood, and could produce a memorable dish from a commonplace larder) by a single three-course lunch.

Readers who are new to Auden might be well advised to plunge into some of the longer works: the immersion is invigorating. Thus, my selection might quite reasonably have simply contained (for example) the ground-breaking charade *Paid on Both Sides*, the engagingly opinionated and autobiographical 'Letter to Lord Byron', the panoramic and moving sonnet-sequence 'In Time of War', the pained and fantastical *ars poetica* 'Caliban to the Audience' from 'The Sea and the Mirror', the Crucifixion sequence 'Horae Canonicae' . . . But I would already have long run out of space, without having offered a single love-lyric or biographical poem, both forms in which Auden was supreme.

Of all possible approaches, I have chosen one which I believe would have pleased him: the 96 pages of text are a little more than two pages for each of the years of his mature writing life, from 1927 to 1973, therefore I have undertaken to include something for every one of those years. Spare pages have gone towards a weighting in the period 1933 to 1939, when his work still seems the most prolific and relevant.

The result, even so, is necessarily a thin spread, but the reader will get a good idea of most of Auden's gifts and obsessions. The lifelong love affair with lead-mining, with its psycho-geological ramifications, can be traced in 'The Watershed', 'England to me is my own tongue' from 'New Year Letter', the songs from *The Age of Anxiety*, and 'In Praise of Limestone'. Response to public events in 1938 ('Here war is simple like a monument') contrasts with response to public events in 1968 ('August 1968'). There are strikingly different approaches, early and late, to such subjects as human knowledge of death ('The Cultural Presupposition' and 'Address to the Beasts'), coming to terms with lost love ('Taller To-day' and 'Since') or the political urgency of choice ('Spain 1937' and 'Aubade'). And of course there are many more complex comparisons across the years to be made between the different forms of poetic analysis and celebration in his work.

Difference there is. Auden was our first major poet to have a scientific education. For him, both Self and Not-Self were infinitely open to whatever clinical approaches the mental laboratory could contrive. Poetic imitation was like a controlled experiment, in which emotions, ideas and beliefs could be tested to breaking-point, and functional variety became itself a test of the poet's social utility.

Auden was a chameleon-like and self-conscious artist, not a Kandinsky but a Picasso, not a Schoenberg but a Stravinsky. You might say that modernism has provided the automobile of literature with a fifth gear, but that post-modernism also likes to get out all the old road maps. In this sense, Auden is also our first post-modernist poet. In the 1930s, in a restless quest for settled belief, he was driven by the investigative and forensic possibilities of all the varied genres, voices and forms of the English poetic tradition. From the 1940s onwards he believed that he had arrived, and so was eventually content to be driven largely by his material.

But he had always been, nonetheless, a poet for whom ideas were crucial; and he never failed to worship the language without whose enchantment ideas in poetry will fail to impress. In his maturity, his poetic ideals were democratic, and for a time he made distinctly greater advances against the commonplace public rejection of modern poetry as difficult, unpleasant and élitist than Yeats or Eliot had managed to do. His aim was 'the thoughts of a wise man in the language of the common people', an impossible ideal that nonetheless made the Auden of the Thirties a household name for apt metaphor, concision and suggestiveness.

What is it we feel we require from an Auden poem? Something political, perhaps, something understated, but dramatic. And accurately coloured with deceptively simple moral observations and quietly charged implications. Something perhaps like 'Gare du Midi' (see p. 30). The station of the title is a Brussels station, the one at which a bureaucrat from Nazi Germany might arrive. 'He walks out briskly to infect a city': before World War One you feared chemical warfare; before World War Two you feared appeasement. The line boldly talks about the one in terms of the other. Mustard gas? Or a diplomat, not with attachés but with a sinister little attaché *case*? The poem itself is like a case. It is a dramatised diplomatic exemplum of a political débâcle.

And yet Auden is not always so simple. The complexities of his thinking and the range of his reading sometimes present syntactic and conceptual hurdles to the reader. If you start reading a late essay-poem like 'The Aliens' (see p. 89) you will soon find yourself thinking that you should perhaps have taken a deeper mental breath before beginning, so as to get through the first six-line sentence at a steady pace. And yet this sentence, though it takes up a variety of related notions in its sweep (our rational relationship with plants and their response to our scientific knowledge, the absolute theological disaster of the Fall, and so on), is no more difficult than it has to be, and is finally not really so difficult after all. Its tone is humorous and tolerant ('the grace of chlorophyll') and restores the sinning Adam for a knowing moment to the innocent garden he once lost.

These are just two sides of a many-sided poet who never failed to remember that poetry must give pleasure. Auden was not often or for long granted personal happiness, but he rarely exploited poetry for the purpose of complaint. In his early poems he recorded a process of alienation, retreat and renewal; in his middle period he encountered the fallible public world that we all create and must inhabit; in his later poems he sought on every occasion for a reason to give thanks. In their different ways these periods are alike in their devotion to the poetic vocation as a sacred trust, and in the conscious choice of perfection of the work over the perfection of the life.

And yet there was for Auden always a danger in poetry becoming too introspective or high-minded. He believed, in a perfectly practical way, that its function was moral and parabolic, and that it could work instructively on any of the many levels at which the human mind functions ('Even a limerick I ought to be something a man of I honour, awaiting death from cancer or a firing squad, I could read without contempt'). In 1936, speaking to the Workers' Educational Association, he put it another way: 'Really to appreciate archdeacons, you must know some barmaids, and vice versa. The same applies to poetry.'

John Fuller

W. H. AUDEN

The Watershed

Who stands, the crux left of the watershed,
On the wet road between the chafing grass
Below him sees dismantled washing-floors,
Snatches of tramline running to the wood,
An industry already comatose,
Yet sparsely living. A ramshackle engine
At Cashwell raises water; for ten years
It lay in flooded workings until this,
Its latter office, grudgingly performed,
And further here and there, though many dead
Lie under the poor soil, some acts are chosen
Taken from recent winters; two there were
Cleaned out a damaged shaft by hand, clutching
The winch the gale would tear them from; one died
During a storm, the fells impassable,
Not at his village, but in wooden shape
Through long abandoned levels nosed his way
And in his final valley went to ground.

Go home, now, stranger, proud of your young stock,
Stranger, turn back again, frustrate and vexed:
This land, cut off, will not communicate,
Be no accessory content to one
Aimless for faces rather there than here.
Beams from your car may cross a bedroom wall,
They wake no sleeper; you may hear the wind
Arriving driven from the ignorant sea
To hurt itself on pane, on bark of elm
Where sap unbaffled rises, being Spring;
But seldom this. Near you, taller than grass,
Ears poise before decision, scenting danger.

The Secret Agent

Control of the passes was, he saw, the key
To this new district, but who would get it?
He, the trained spy, had walked into the trap
For a bogus guide, seduced with the old tricks.

At Greenhearth was a fine site for a dam
And easy power, had they pushed the rail
Some stations nearer. They ignored his wires.
The bridges were unbuilt and trouble coming.

The street music seemed gracious now to one
For weeks up in the desert. Woken by water
Running away in the dark, he often had
Reproached the night for a companion
Dreamed of already. They would shoot, of course,
Parting easily who were never joined.

Taller To-day

Taller to-day, we remember similar evenings,
Walking together in the windless orchard
Where the brook runs over the gravel, far from the glacier.

Again in the room with the sofa hiding the grate,
Look down to the river when the rain is over,
See him turn to the window, hearing our last
Of Captain Ferguson.

It is seen how excellent hands have turned to commonness.
One staring too long, went blind in a tower,
One sold all his manors to fight, broke through, and faltered.

Nights come bringing the snow, and the dead howl
Under the headlands in their windy dwelling
Because the Adversary put too easy questions
On lonely roads.

But happy now, though no nearer each other,
We see the farms lighted all along the valley;
Down at the mill-shed the hammering stops
And men go home.

Noises at dawn will bring
Freedom for some, but not this peace
No bird can contradict: passing, but is sufficient now
For something fulfilled this hour, loved or endured.

Shut Your Eyes and Open Your Mouth

Sentries against inner and outer,
At stated interval is feature;
And how shall enemy on these
Make sudden raid or lasting peace?
For bribery were vain to try
Against the incorruptible eye
Too amply paid with tears, the chin
Has hairs to hide its weakness in,
And proud bridge and indignant nostril
Nothing to do but to look noble.
But in between these lies the mouth;
Watch that, that you may parley with:
There strategy comes easiest,
Though it seem stern, was seen compressed
Over a lathe, refusing answer,
It will release the ill-fed prisoner,
It will do murder or betray
For either party equally,
Yielding at last to a close kiss
It will admit tongue's soft advance,
So longed for, given in abandon,
Given long since, had it but known.

This Lunar Beauty

This lunar beauty
Has no history
Is complete and early;
If beauty later
Bear any feature
It had a lover
And is another.

This like a dream
Keeps other time
And daytime is
The loss of this;
For time is inches
And the heart's changes
Where ghost has haunted
Lost and wanted.

But this was never
A ghost's endeavour
Nor finished this,
Was ghost at ease;
And till it pass
Love shall not near
The sweetness here
Nor sorrow take
His endless look.

Argument, Part iii

Came one after a ruined harvest, with a schoolroom globe, a wizard, sorry. From the nipping North Righteousness running. But where that warm boy of the summer château? Found on wet roads early this morning, patches of oil, the face of an avenger, downwards. Speech of worn tools in a box, thoughts from the trap.

Sound of guns in the city, the voice of the demonstrator, 'Gentlemen, to-morrow we shall tie the carotid.' What memory of self-regard from the locked room, shaken by lorries, from the depressed areas?

Suspicion of one of our number, away for week-ends. Catching sight of Him on the lawn with the gardener, from the upper rooms of a house. His insane dislike of birds. His fondness for verbal puzzles. Friendly joking converting itself into a counterplot, the spore of fear. Then in the hot weeks, the pavement blistering and the press muzzled, the sudden disaster, surprising as a comic turn. Shutting the door on the machines, we stood in the silence, thinking of nothing. (Murder of a rook by weasels.) Some taking refuge in thankful disillusion, others in frank disbelief, the youngest getting drunk. Hysterical attempts of two women to reach Him. The slow seeping in of their sly condolences, of the mass hatred of the villas. A child's sense of failure after burning a slug in a candle.

Daylight, striking at the eye from far-off roofs, why did you blind us, think: we who on the snow-line were in love with death, despised vegetation, we forgot His will; who came to us in an extraordinary dream, calming the plunging dangerous horses, greeting our arrival on a reedy shore. His sharing from His own provisions after the blizzard's march. The thrashing He gave the dishonest contractor who promised marvels in an old boy's tie. The old peasant couple's belief in His magical powers. His ability to smell a wet knife at a distance of half a mile. His refusal to wear anything but silk next to His skin. His reverent stories of the underpaid drunken usher who taught Him all. His tale of the Three Sorb Trees. His words after we had failed Him at the Roman bridge.

Love, that notable forked one, riding away from the farm, the ill word said, fought at the frozen dam, transforms itself to influenza and guilty rashes. Seduction of a postmistress on the lead roof of a church-tower, and an immature boy wrapping himself in a towel, ashamed at the public baths. From these stony acres, a witless generation, plant-like in beauty.

On the steps of His stone the boys play prisoner's base, turning their backs on the inscription, unconscious of sorrow as the sea of drowning. Passage to music of an unchaste hero from a too-strict country. March, long black piano, silhouetted head; cultured daughter of a greying ironmaster, march through fields. The hammer settles on the white-hot ingot. The telescope focuses accurately upon a recent star. On skyline of detritus, a truck, nose up. Loiterer at carved gates, immune stranger, follow. It is nothing, your loss. The priest's mouth opens in the green graveyard, but the wind is against it.

Epilogue

'O where are you going?' said reader to rider,
'That valley is fatal where furnaces burn,
Yonder's the midden whose odours will madden,
That gap is the grave where the tall return.'

'O do you imagine', said fearer to farer,
'That dusk will delay on your path to the pass,
Your diligent looking discover the lacking
Your footsteps feel from granite to grass?'

'O what was that bird', said horror to hearer,
'Did you see that shape in the twisted trees?
Behind you swiftly the figure comes softly,
The spot on your skin is a shocking disease?'

'Out of this house' – said rider to reader
'Yours never will' – said farer to fearer
'They're looking for you' – said hearer to horror
As he left them there, as he left them there.

Getting Dressed

Now picking from chair, I passed over head
The loose-fitting shirt of light flannel,
Pickle-red from soaking in a secret die
Distilled from coal-tar, the exact shade
Calculated in a notebook, known before seen
By men to whom thermometers are more than women.
Wound round neck the wort-blue tie,
Knotting at the windpipe in a neat bow.
Then I pulled on the hairy breeches
Smelling of peat from skua-breeding Harris,
Caught round the waist with a calf-leather belt
That joined at the navel with a nickel clip,
And in the region which is touched for the reflex of the knee
Fastened with tabs. Took from drawer
The closely-woven mudproof stockings,
Carried from corner the climber's boots,
Polished with grease and pride of craftsman,
Hand-made in rainy Esthwaite to last a lifetime,
Studded on the soles in concentric horseshoes
With three-pronged nails, and now beginning
At the middle of the instep from ankle to knee
Carefully the spiral khaki puttees
I wound and fastened; fetched the jacket
Matching the breeches, and the motorist's cap;
Shook out a handkerchief of Irish linen
And started downstairs to find my friend.

O What is That Sound

O what is that sound which so thrills the ear
    Down in the valley drumming, drumming?
Only the scarlet soldiers, dear,
        The soldiers coming.

O what is that light I see flashing so clear
    Over the distance brightly, brightly?
Only the sun on their weapons, dear,
        As they step lightly.

O what are they doing with all that gear;
    What are they doing this morning, this morning?
Only the usual manœuvres, dear,
        Or perhaps a warning.

O why have they left the road down there;
    Why are they suddenly wheeling, wheeling?
Perhaps a change in the orders, dear;
        Why are you kneeling?

O haven't they stopped for the doctor's care;
    Haven't they reined their horses, their horses?
Why, they are none of them wounded, dear,
        None of these forces.

O is it the parson they want with white hair;
    Is it the parson, is it, is it?
No, they are passing his gateway, dear,
        Without a visit.

O it must be the farmer who lives so near;
    It must be the farmer so cunning, so cunning?
They have passed the farm already, dear,
        And now they are running.

O where are you going? stay with me here!
    Were the vows you swore me deceiving, deceiving?
No, I promised to love you, dear,
        But I must be leaving.

O it's broken the lock and splintered the door,
    O it's the gate where they're turning, turning;
Their feet are heavy on the floor
        And their eyes are burning.

A Summer Night
(*To Geoffrey Hoyland*)

Out on the lawn I lie in bed,
Vega conspicuous overhead
   In the windless nights of June;
Forests of green have done complete
The day's activity; my feet
   Point to the rising moon.

Lucky, this point in time and space
Is chosen as my working place;
   Where the sexy airs of summer,
The bathing hours and the bare arms,
The leisured drives through a land of farms,
   Are good to the newcomer.

Equal with colleagues in a ring
I sit on each calm evening,
   Enchanted as the flowers
The opening light draws out of hiding
From leaves with all its dove-like pleading
   Its logic and its powers.

That later we, though parted then
May still recall these evenings when
   Fear gave his watch no look;
The lion griefs loped from the shade
And on our knees their muzzles laid,
   And Death put down his book.

Moreover, eyes in which I learn
That I am glad to look, return
   My glances every day;
And when the birds and rising sun
Waken me, I shall speak with one
   Who has not gone away.

Now North and South and East and West
Those I love lie down to rest;
    The moon looks on them all:
The healers and the brilliant talkers,
The eccentrics and the silent walkers,
    The dumpy and the tall.

She climbs the European sky;
Churches and power stations lie
    Alike among earth's fixtures:
Into the galleries she peers,
And blankly as an orphan stares
    Upon the marvellous pictures.

To gravity attentive, she
Can notice nothing here; though we
    Whom hunger cannot move,
From gardens where we feel secure
Look up, and with a sigh endure
    The tyrannies of love:

And, gentle, do not care to know,
Where Poland draws her Eastern bow,
    What violence is done;
Nor ask what doubtful act allows
Our freedom in this English house,
    Our picnics in the sun.

The creepered wall stands up to hide
The gathering multitudes outside
    Whose glances hunger worsens;
Concealing from their wretchedness
Our metaphysical distress,
    Our kindness to ten persons.

And now no path on which we move
But shows already traces of
    Intentions not our own,

Thoroughly able to achieve
What our excitement could conceive,
    But our hands left alone.

For what by nature and by training
We loved, has little strength remaining:
    Though we would gladly give
The Oxford colleges, Big Ben,
And all the birds in Wicken Fen,
    It has no wish to live.

Soon through the dykes of our content
The crumpling flood will force a rent,
    And, taller than a tree,
Hold sudden death before our eyes
Whose river-dreams long hid the size
    And vigours of the sea.

But when the waters make retreat
And through the black mud first the wheat
    In shy green stalks appears;
When stranded monsters gasping lie,
And sounds of riveting terrify
    Their whorled unsubtle ears:

May this for which we dread to lose
Our privacy, need no excuse
    But to that strength belong;
As through a child's rash happy cries
The drowned voices of his parents rise
    In unlamenting song.

After discharges of alarm,
All unpredicted may it calm
    The pulse of nervous nations;
Forgive the murderer in his glass,
Tough in its patience to surpass
    The tigress her swift motions.

'May with its light behaving'

May with its light behaving
Stirs vessel, eye, and limb;
The singular and sad
Are willing to recover,
And to the swan-delighting river
The careless picnics come,
The living white and red.

The dead remote and hooded
In their enclosures rest; but we
From the vague woods have broken,
Forests where children meet
And the white angel-vampires flit;
We stand with shaded eye,
The dangerous apple taken.

The real world lies before us;
Animal motions of the young,
The common wish for death,
The pleasured and the haunted;
The dying master sinks tormented
In the admirers' ring,
The unjust walk the earth.

And love that makes impatient
The tortoise and the roe, and lays
The blonde beside the dark,
Urges upon our blood,
Before the evil and the good
How insufficient is
The endearment and the look.

The Cultural Presupposition

Happy the hare at morning, for she cannot read
The Hunter's waking thoughts. Lucky the leaf
Unable to predict the fall. Lucky indeed
The rampant suffering suffocating jelly
Burgeoning in pools, lapping the grits of the desert:
The elementary sensual cures,
The hibernations and the growth of hair assuage:
Or best of all the mineral stars disintegrating quietly into
                                                    light
But what shall man do, who can whistle tunes by heart,
Know to the bar when death shall cut him short, like the cry
                                        of the shearwater?
We will show you what he has done.
How comely are his places of refuge and the tabernacles of
                                                his peace,
The new books upon the morning table, the lawns and the
                                        afternoon terraces!
Here are the playing-fields where he may forget his ignorance
To operate within a gentleman's agreement: twenty-two sins
                                        have here a certain licence.
Here are the thickets where accosted lovers combatant
May warm each other with their wicked hands,
Here are the avenues for incantation and workshops for the
                                        cunning engravers.
The galleries are full of music, the pianist is storming the
    keys, the great cellist is crucified over his instrument,
That none may hear the ejaculations of the sentinels
Nor the sigh of the most numerous and the most poor; the
                                        thud of their falling bodies
Who with their lives have banished hence the serpent and the
                                        faceless insect.

On This Island

Look, stranger, at this island now
The leaping light for your delight discovers,
Stand stable here
And silent be,
That through the channels of the ear
May wander like a river
The swaying sound of the sea.

Here at the small field's ending pause
Where the chalk wall falls to the foam, and its tall ledges
Oppose the pluck
And knock of the tide,
And the shingle scrambles after the suck-
ing surf, and the gull lodges
A moment on its sheer side.

Far off like floating seeds the ships
Diverge on urgent voluntary errands;
And the full view
Indeed may enter
And move in memory as now these clouds do,
That pass the harbour mirror
And all the summer through the water saunter.

'Fish in the unruffled lakes'

Fish in the unruffled lakes
The swarming colours wear,
Swans in the winter air
A white perfection have,
And the great lion walks
Through his innocent grove;
Lion, fish, and swan
Act, and are gone
Upon Time's toppling wave.

We till shadowed days are done,
We must weep and sing
Duty's conscious wrong,
The devil in the clock,
The Goodness carefully worn
For atonement or for luck;
We must lose our loves,
On each beast and bird that moves
Turn an envious look.

Sighs for folly said and done
Twist our narrow days;
But I must bless, I must praise
That you, my swan, who have
All gifts that to the swan
Impulsive Nature gave,
The majesty and pride,
Last night should add
Your voluntary love.

Funeral Blues

Stop all the clocks, cut off the telephone,
Prevent the dog from barking with a juicy bone,
Silence the pianos and with muffled drum
Bring out the coffin, let the mourners come.

Let aeroplanes circle moaning overhead
Scribbling on the sky the message He Is Dead,
Put crêpe bows round the white necks of the public doves,
Let the traffic policemen wear black cotton gloves.

He was my North, my South, my East and West,
My working week and my Sunday rest,
My noon, my midnight, my talk, my song;
I thought that love would last for ever: I was wrong.

The stars are not wanted now; put out every one,
Pack up the moon and dismantle the sun,
Pour away the ocean and sweep up the wood;
For nothing now can ever come to any good.

Detective Story

For who is ever quite without his landscape,
The straggling village street, the house in trees,
All near the church, or else the gloomy town house,
The one with the Corinthian pillars, or
The tiny workmanlike flat: in any case
A home, the centre where the three or four things
That happen to a man do happen? Yes,
Who cannot draw the map of his life, shade in
The little station where he meets his loves
And says good-bye continually, and mark the spot
Where the body of his happiness was first discovered?

An unknown tramp? A rich man? An enigma always
And with a buried past – but when the truth,
The truth about our happiness comes out
How much it owed to blackmail and philandering.

The rest's traditional. All goes to plan:
The feud between the local common sense
And that exasperating brilliant intuition
That's always on the spot by chance before us;
All goes to plan, both lying and confession,
Down to the thrilling final chase, the kill.

Yet on the last page just a lingering doubt
That verdict, was it just? The judge's nerves,
That clue, that protestation from the gallows,
And our own smile . . . why yes . . .
But time is always killed. Someone must pay for
Our loss of happiness, our happiness itself.

Spain 1937

Yesterday all the past. The language of size
Spreading to China along the trade-routes; the diffusion
        Of the counting-frame and the cromlech;
Yesterday the shadow-reckoning in the sunny climates.

Yesterday the assessment of insurance by cards,
The divination of water; yesterday the invention
        Of cart-wheels and clocks, the taming of
Horses; yesterday the bustling world of the navigators.

Yesterday the abolition of fairies and giants;
The fortress like a motionless eagle eyeing the valley,
        The chapel built in the forest;
Yesterday the carving of angels and of frightening gargoyles;

The trial of heretics among the columns of stone;
Yesterday the theological feuds in the taverns
        And the miraculous cure at the fountain;
Yesterday the Sabbath of Witches. But to-day the struggle.

Yesterday the installation of dynamos and turbines;
The construction of railways in the colonial desert;
        Yesterday the classic lecture
On the origin of Mankind. But to-day the struggle.

Yesterday the belief in the absolute value of Greek;
The fall of the curtain upon the death of a hero;
        Yesterday the prayer to the sunset
And the adoration of madmen. But to-day the struggle.

As the poet whispers, startled among the pines
Or, where the loose waterfall sings, compact, or upright
        On the crag by the leaning tower:
'O my vision. O send me the luck of the sailor.'

And the investigator peers through his instruments
At the inhuman provinces, the virile bacillus
          Or enormous Jupiter finished:
'But the lives of my friends. I inquire, I inquire.'

And the poor in their fireless lodgings dropping the sheets
Of the evening paper: 'Our day is our loss. O show us
          History the operator, the
Organiser, Time the refreshing river.'

And the nations combine each cry, invoking the life
That shapes the individual belly and orders
          The private nocturnal terror:
'Did you not found once the city state of the sponge,

'Raise the vast military empires of the shark
And the tiger, establish the robin's plucky canton?
          Intervene. O descend as a dove or
A furious papa or a mild engineer: but descend.'

And the life, if it answers at all, replies from the heart
And the eyes and the lungs, from the shops and squares of
                                                    the city:
          'O no, I am not the Mover,
Not to-day, not to you. To you I'm the

'Yes-man, the bar-companion, the easily-duped:
I am whatever you do; I am your vow to be
          Good, your humorous story;
I am your business voice; I am your marriage.

'What's your proposal? To build the Just City? I will.
I agree. Or is it the suicide pact, the romantic
          Death? Very well, I accept, for
I am your choice, your decision: yes, I am Spain.'

Many have heard it on remote peninsulas,
On sleepy plains, in the aberrant fishermen's islands,
          In the corrupt heart of the city;
Have heard and migrated like gulls or the seeds of a flower.

They clung like burrs to the long expresses that lurch
Through the unjust lands, through the night, through the
alpine tunnel;
They floated over the oceans;
They walked the passes: they came to present their lives.

On that arid square, that fragment nipped off from hot
Africa, soldered so crudely to inventive Europe,
On that tableland scored by rivers,
Our fever's menacing shapes are precise and alive.

To-morrow, perhaps, the future: the research on fatigue
And the movements of packers; the gradual exploring of all
the
Octaves of radiation;
To-morrow the enlarging of consciousness by diet and
breathing.

To-morrow the rediscovery of romantic love;
The photographing of ravens; all the fun under
Liberty's masterful shadow;
To-morrow the hour of the pageant-master and the
musician.

To-morrow for the young the poets exploding like bombs,
The walks by the lake, the winter of perfect communion;
To-morrow the bicycle races
Through the suburbs on summer evenings: but to-day the
struggle.

To-day the inevitable increase in the chances of death;
The conscious acceptance of guilt in the fact of murder;
To-day the expending of powers
On the flat ephemeral pamphlet and the boring meeting.

To-day the makeshift consolations; the shared cigarette;
The cards in the candle-lit barn and the scraping concert,
The masculine jokes; to-day the
Fumbled and unsatisfactory embrace before hurting.

The stars are dead; the animals will not look:
We are left alone with our day, and the time is short and
            History to the defeated
May say Alas but cannot help or pardon.

The Sphinx

Did it once issue from the carver's hand
Healthy? Even the earliest conquerors saw
The face of a sick ape, a bandaged paw,
A Presence in the hot invaded land.

The lion of a tortured stubborn star,
It does not like the young, nor love, nor learning:
Time hurt it like a person; it lies, turning
A vast behind on shrill America,

And witnesses. The huge hurt face accuses,
And pardons nothing, least of all success.
The answers that it utters have no uses

To those who face akimbo its distress:
'Do people like me?' No. The slave amuses
The lion: 'Am I to suffer always?' Yes.

'Here war is simple like a monument'

Here war is simple like a monument:
A telephone is speaking to a man;
Flags on a map assert that troops were sent;
A boy brings milk in bowls. There is a plan

For living men in terror of their lives,
Who thirst at nine who were to thirst at noon,
And can be lost and are, and miss their wives,
And, unlike an idea, can die too soon.

But ideas can be true although men die,
And we can watch a thousand faces
Made active by one lie:

And maps can really point to places
Where life is evil now:
Nanking; Dachau.

Musée des Beaux Arts

About suffering they were never wrong,
The Old Masters: how well they understood
Its human position; how it takes place
While someone else is eating or opening a window or just
                              walking dully along;
How, when the aged are reverently, passionately waiting
For the miraculous birth, there always must be
Children who did not specially want it to happen, skating
On a pond at the edge of the wood:
They never forgot
That even the dreadful martyrdom must run its course
Anyhow in a corner, some untidy spot
Where the dogs go on with their doggy life and the torturer's
                              horse
Scratches its innocent behind on a tree.

In Brughel's *Icarus*, for instance: how everything turns away
Quite leisurely from the disaster; the ploughman may
Have heard the splash, the forsaken cry,
But for him it was not an important failure; the sun shone
As it had to on the white legs disappearing into the green
Water; and the expensive delicate ship that must have seen
Something amazing, a boy falling out of the sky,
Had somewhere to get to and sailed calmly on.

Gare du Midi

A nondescript express in from the South,
Crowds round the ticket barrier, a face
To welcome which the mayor has not contrived
Bugles or braid: something about the mouth
Distracts the stray look with alarm and pity.
Snow is falling. Clutching a little case,
He walks out briskly to infect a city
Whose terrible future may have just arrived.

Refugee Blues

Say this city has ten million souls,
Some are living in mansions, some are living in holes:
Yet there's no place for us, my dear, yet there's no place for
us.

Once we had a country and we thought it fair,
Look in the atlas and you'll find it there:
We cannot go there now, my dear, we cannot go there now.

In the village churchyard there grows an old yew,
Every spring it blossoms anew:
Old passports can't do that, my dear, old passports can't do
that.

The consul banged the table and said:
'If you've got no passport you're officially dead':
But we are still alive, my dear, but we are still alive.

Went to a committee; they offered me a chair;
Asked me politely to return next year:
But where shall we go to-day, my dear, but where shall we go
to-day?

Came to a public meeting; the speaker got up and said:
'If we let them in, they will steal our daily bread';
He was talking of you and me, my dear, he was talking of you
and me.

Thought I heard the thunder rumbling in the sky;
It was Hitler over Europe, saying: 'They must die';
We were in his mind, my dear, we were in his mind.

Saw a poodle in a jacket fastened with a pin,
Saw a door opened and a cat let in:
But they weren't German Jews, my dear, but they weren't
German Jews.

Went down to the harbour and stood upon the quay,
Saw the fish swimming as if they were free:
Only ten feet away, my dear, only ten feet away.

Walked through a wood, saw the birds in the trees;
They had no politicians and sang at their ease:
They weren't the human race, my dear, they weren't the
                                              human race.

Dreamed I saw a building with a thousand floors,
A thousand windows and a thousand doors;
Not one of them was ours, my dear, not one of them was
                                              ours.

Stood on a great plain in the falling snow;
Ten thousand soldiers marched to and fro:
Looking for you and me, my dear, looking for you and me.

In Memory of W. B. Yeats
(d. Jan. 1939)

1

He disappeared in the dead of winter:
The brooks were frozen, the air-ports almost deserted,
And snow disfigured the public statues;
The mercury sank in the mouth of the dying day.
O all the instruments agree
The day of his death was a dark cold day.

Far from his illness
The wolves ran on through the evergreen forests,
The peasant river was untempted by the fashionable quays;
By mourning tongues
The death of the poet was kept from his poems.

But for him it was his last afternoon as himself,
An afternoon of nurses and rumours;
The provinces of his body revolted,
The squares of his mind were empty,
Silence invaded the suburbs,
The current of his feeling failed: he became his admirers.

Now he is scattered among a hundred cities
And wholly given over to unfamiliar affections;
To find his happiness in another kind of wood
And be punished under a foreign code of conscience.
The words of a dead man
Are modified in the guts of the living.

But in the importance and noise of to-morrow
When the brokers are roaring like beasts on the floor of the
                                                            Bourse,
And the poor have the sufferings to which they are fairly
                                                            accustomed,

And each in the cell of himself is almost convinced of his
                                                          freedom;
A few thousand will think of this day
As one thinks of a day when one did something slightly
                                                          unusual.

O all the instruments agree
The day of his death was a dark cold day.

2

You were silly like us: your gift survived it all;
The parish of rich women, physical decay,
Yourself; mad Ireland hurt you into poetry.
Now Ireland has her madness and her weather still,
For poetry makes nothing happen: it survives
In the valley of its saying where executives
Would never want to tamper; it flows south
From ranches of isolation and the busy griefs,
Raw towns that we believe and die in; it survives,
A way of happening, a mouth.

3

Earth, receive an honoured guest;
William Yeats is laid to rest:
Let the Irish vessel lie
Emptied of its poetry.

Time that is intolerant
Of the brave and innocent,
And indifferent in a week
To a beautiful physique,

Worships language and forgives
Everyone by whom it lives;
Pardons cowardice, conceit,
Lays its honours at their feet.

Time that with this strange excuse
Pardoned Kipling and his views,
And will pardon Paul Claudel,
Pardons him for writing well.

In the nightmare of the dark
All the dogs of Europe bark,
And the living nations wait,
Each sequestered in its hate;

Intellectual disgrace
Stares from every human face,
And the seas of pity lie
Locked and frozen in each eye.

Follow, poet, follow right
To the bottom of the night,
With your unconstraining voice
Still persuade us to rejoice;

With the farming of a verse
Make a vineyard of the curse,
Sing of human unsuccess
In a rapture of distress;

In the deserts of the heart
Let the healing fountain start,
In the prison of his days
Teach the free man how to praise.

Epitaph on a Tyrant

Perfection, of a kind, was what he was after,
And the poetry he invented was easy to understand;
He knew human folly like the back of his hand,
And was greatly interested in armies and fleets;
When he laughed, respectable senators burst with laughter,
And when he cried the little children died in the streets.

'Carry her over the water'

Carry her over the water,
    And set her down under the tree,
Where the culvers white all day and all night,
    And the winds from every quarter,
Sing agreeably, agreeably, agreeably of love.

Put a gold ring on her finger,
    And press her close to your heart,
While the fish in the lake their snapshots take,
    And the frog, that sanguine singer,
Sings agreeably, agreeably, agreeably of love.

The streets shall all flock to your marriage,
    The houses turn round to look,
The tables and chairs say suitable prayers,
    And the horses drawing your carriage
Sing agreeably, agreeably, agreeably of love.

'England to me is my own tongue'

England to me is my own tongue,
And what I did when I was young.
If now, two aliens in New York,
We meet, Elizabeth , and talk
Of friends who suffer in the torn
Old Europe where we both were born,
What this refutes or that confirms,
I can but think our talk in terms
Of images that I have seen,
And England tells me what we mean.
Thus, squalid beery BURTON stands
For shoddy thinking of all brands;
The wreck of RHONDDA for the mess
We make when for a short success
We split our symmetry apart,
Deny the Reason or the Heart;
YE OLDë TUDOR TEA-SHOPPE for
The folly of dogmatic law,
While graceless BOURNEMOUTH is the sloth
Of men or bureaucrats or both.

No matter where, or whom I meet,
Shop-gazing in a Paris street,
Bumping through Iceland in a bus,
At teas where clubwomen discuss
The latest Federation Plan,
In Pullman washrooms, man to man,
Hearing how circumstance has vexed
A broker who is oversexed,
In houses where they do not drink,
Whenever I begin to think
About the human creature we
Must nurse to sense and decency,

An English area comes to mind,
I see the nature of my kind
As a locality I love,
Those limestone moors that stretch from BROUGH
To HEXHAM and the ROMAN WALL,
There is my symbol of us all.
There, where the EDEN leisures through
Its sandstone valley, is my view
Of green and civil life that dwells
Below a cliff of savage fells
From which original address
Man faulted into consciousness.
Along the line of lapse the fire
Of life's impersonal desire
Burst through his sedentary rock
And, as at DUFTON and at KNOCK,
Thrust up between his mind and heart
Enormous cones of myth and art.
Always my boy of wish returns
To those peat-stained deserted burns
That feed the WEAR and TYNE and TEES,
And, turning states to strata, sees
How basalt long oppressed broke out
In wild revolt at CAULDRON SNOUT,
And from the relics of old mines
Derives his algebraic signs
For all in man that mourns and seeks,
For all of his renounced techniques,
Their tramways overgrown with grass,
For lost belief, for all Alas,
The derelict lead-smelting mill,
Flued to its chimney up the hill,
That smokes no answer any more
But points, a landmark on BOLTS LAW,
The finger of all questions. There
In ROOKHOPE I was first aware

Of Self and Not-self, Death and Dread:
Adits were entrances which led
Down to the Outlawed, to the Others,
The Terrible, the Merciful, the Mothers;
Alone in the hot day I knelt
Upon the edge of shafts and felt
The deep *Urmutterfurcht* that drives
Us into knowledge all our lives,
The far interior of our fate
To civilise and to create,
Das Weibliche that bids us come
To find what we're escaping from.
There I dropped pebbles, listened, heard
The reservoir of darkness stirred;
'*O deine Mutter kehrt dir nicht*
Wieder. Du selbst bin ich, dein' Pflicht
Und Liebe. Brach sie nun mein Bild.'
And I was conscious of my guilt.

If I Could Tell You

Time will say nothing but I told you so,
Time only knows the price we have to pay;
If I could tell you I would let you know.

If we should weep when clowns put on their show,
If we should stumble when musicians play,
Time will say nothing but I told you so.

There are no fortunes to be told, although,
Because I love you more than I can say,
If I could tell you I would let you know.

The winds must come from somewhere when they blow,
There must be reasons why the leaves decay;
Time will say nothing but I told you so.

Perhaps the roses really want to grow,
The vision seriously intends to stay;
If I could tell you I would let you know.

Suppose the lions all get up and go,
And all the brooks and soldiers run away;
Will Time say nothing but I told you so?
If I could tell you I would let you know.

Atlantis

Being set on the idea
    Of getting to Atlantis,
You have discovered of course
    Only the Ship of Fools is
Making the voyage this year,
As gales of abnormal force
    Are predicted, and that you
    Must therefore be ready to
Behave absurdly enough
    To pass for one of The Boys,
At least appearing to love
    Hard liquor, horseplay and noise.

Should storms, as may well happen,
    Drive you to anchor a week
In some old harbour-city
    Of Ionia, then speak
With her witty scholars, men
Who have proved there cannot be
    Such a place as Atlantis:
    Learn their logic, but notice
How their subtlety betrays
    A simple enormous grief;
Thus they shall teach you the ways
    To doubt that you may believe.

If, later, you run aground
    Among the headlands of Thrace
Where with torches all night long
    A naked barbaric race
Leaps frenziedly to the sound
Of conch and dissonant gong;
    On that stony savage shore
    Strip off your clothes and dance, for

Unless you are capable
   Of forgetting completely
About Atlantis, you will
   Never finish your journey.

Again, should you come to gay
   Carthage or Corinth, take part
In their endless gaiety;
   And if in some bar a tart,
As she strokes your hair, should say
'This is Atlantis, dearie,'
   Listen with attentiveness
   To her life-story: unless
You become acquainted now
   With each refuge that tries to
Counterfeit Atlantis, how
   Will you recognize the true?

Assuming you beach at last
   Near Atlantis, and begin
The terrible trek inland
   Through squalid woods and frozen
Tundras where all are soon lost;
If, forsaken then, you stand,
   Dismissal everywhere,
   Stone and snow, silence and air,
Remember the noble dead
   And honour the fate you are,
Travelling and tormented,
   Dialectic and bizarre.

Stagger onward rejoicing;
   And even then if, perhaps
Having actually got
   To the last col, you collapse
With all Atlantis gleaming
Below you yet you cannot

Descend, you should still be proud
    Even to have been allowed
Just to peep at Atlantis
    In a poetic vision:
Give thanks and lie down in peace,
    Having seen your salvation.

All the little household gods
    Have started crying, but say
Good-bye now, and put to sea.
    Farewell, dear friend, farewell: may
Hermes, master of the roads
And the four dwarf Kabiri,
    Protect and serve you always;
    And may the Ancient of Days
Provide for all you must do
    His invisible guidance,
Lifting up, friend, upon you
    The light of His countenance.

The Lesson

The first time that I dreamed, we were in flight,
And fagged with running; there was civil war,
A valley full of thieves and wounded bears.

Farms blazed behind us; turning to the right,
We came at once to a tall house, its door
Wide open, waiting for its long-lost heirs.

An elderly clerk sat on the bedroom stairs
Writing; but we had tiptoed past him when
He raised his head and stuttered – 'Go away'.

We wept and begged to stay:
He wiped his pince-nez, hesitated, then
Said no, he had no power to give us leave;
Our lives were not in order; we must leave.

*

The second dream began in a May wood;
We had been laughing; your blue eyes were kind,
Your excellent nakedness without disdain.

Our lips met, wishing universal good;
But, on their impact, sudden flame and wind
Fetched you away and turned me loose again

To make a focus for a wide wild plain,
Dead level and dead silent and bone dry,
Where nothing could have suffered, sinned, or grown.
On a high chair alone
I sat, a little master, asking why
The cold and solid object in my hands
Should be a human hand, one of your hands.

*

And the last dream was this: we were to go
To a great banquet and a Victory Ball
After some tournament or dangerous test.

Our cushions were of crimson velvet, so
We must have won; though there were crowns for all,
Ours were of gold, of paper all the rest.

Fair, wise or funny was each famous guest,
Love smiled at Courage over priceless glass,
And rockets died in hundreds to express
Our learned carelessness.
A band struck up; all over the green grass
A sea of paper crowns rose up to dance:
Ours were too heavy; we did not dance.

*

I woke. You were not there. But as I dressed
Anxiety turned to shame, feeling all three
Intended one rebuke. For had not each
In its own way tried to teach
My will to love you that it cannot be,
As I think, of such consequence to want
What anyone is given, if they want?

Miranda's Song

My Dear One is mine as mirrors are lonely,
As the poor and sad are real to the good king,
And the high green hill sits always by the sea.

Up jumped the Black Man behind the elder tree,
Turned a somersault and ran away waving;
My Dear One is mine as mirrors are lonely.

The Witch gave a squawk; her venomous body
Melted into light as water leaves a spring,
And the high green hill sits always by the sea.

At his crossroads, too, the Ancient prayed for me;
Down his wasted cheeks tears of joy were running:
My Dear One is mine as mirrors are lonely.

He kissed me awake, and no one was sorry;
The sun shone on sails, eyes, pebbles, anything,
And the high green hill sits always by the sea.

So, to remember our changing garden, we
Are linked as children in a circle dancing:
My Dear One is mine as mirrors are lonely,
And the high green hill sits always by the sea.

'As yet the young hero's'

As yet the young hero's
Brow is unkissed by battle,
But he knows how necessary
Is his defiance of fate
And, serene already, he sails
Down the gorge between the august
Faces carved in the cliffs
Towards the lordship of the world.

And the gentle majority are not
Afraid either, but, owl-like
And sedate in their glass globes
The wedded couples wave
At the bandits racing by
With affection, and the learned relax
On pinguid plains among
A swarm of flying flowers.

But otherwise is it with the play
Of the child whom chance decrees
To say what all men suffer:
For he wishes against his will
To be lost, and his fear leads him
To dales of driving rain
Where peasants with penthouse eyebrows
Sullenly guard the sluices.

And his steps follow the stream
Past rusting apparatus
To its gloomy beginning, the original
Chasm where brambles block
The entrance to the underworld;
There the silence blesses his sorrow,
And holy to his dread is that dark
Which will neither promise nor explain.

Prospector's Ballad

When Laura lay on her ledger side
And nicely threw her north cheek up,
How pleasing the plight of her promising grove
And how rich the random I reached with a rise.

The Fall of Rome

(*for Cyril Connolly*)

The piers are pummelled by the waves;
In a lonely field the rain
Lashes an abandoned train;
Outlaws fill the mountain caves.

Fantastic grow the evening gowns;
Agents of the Fisc pursue
Absconding tax-defaulters through
The sewers of provincial towns.

Private rites of magic send
The temple prostitutes to sleep;
All the literati keep
An imaginary friend.

Cerebrotonic Cato may
Extol the Ancient Disciplines,
But the muscle-bound Marines
Mutiny for food and pay.

Caesar's double-bed is warm
As an unimportant clerk
Writes *I DO NOT LIKE MY WORK*
On a pink official form.

Unendowed with wealth or pity,
Little birds with scarlet legs,
Sitting on their speckled eggs,
Eye each flu-infected city.

Altogether elsewhere, vast
Herds of reindeer move across
Miles and miles of golden moss,
Silently and very fast.

In Praise of Limestone

If it form the one landscape that we, the inconstant ones,
    Are consistently homesick for, this is chiefly
Because it dissolves in water. Mark these rounded slopes
    With their surface fragrance of thyme and, beneath,
A secret system of caves and conduits; hear the springs
    That spurt out everywhere with a chuckle,
Each filling a private pool for its fish and carving
    Its own little ravine whose cliffs entertain
The butterfly and the lizard; examine this region
    Of short distances and definite places:
What could be more like Mother or a fitter background
    For her son, the flirtatious male who lounges
Against a rock in the sunlight, never doubting
    That for all his faults he is loved; whose works are but
Extensions of his power to charm? From weathered outcrop
    To hill-top temple, from appearing waters to
Conspicuous fountains, from a wild to a formal vineyard,
    Are ingenious but short steps that a child's wish
To receive more attention than his brothers, whether
    By pleasing or teasing, can easily take.

Watch, then, the band of rivals as they climb up and down
    Their steep stone gennels in twos and threes, at times
Arm in arm, but never, thank God, in step; or engaged
    On the shady side of a square at midday in
Voluble discourse, knowing each other too well to think
    There are any important secrets, unable
To conceive a god whose temper-tantrums are moral
    And not to be pacified by a clever line
Or a good lay: for, accustomed to a stone that responds,
    They have never had to veil their faces in awe
Of a crater whose blazing fury could not be fixed;
    Adjusted to the local needs of valleys

Where everything can be touched or reached by walking,
    Their eyes have never looked into infinite space
Through the lattice-work of a nomad's comb; born lucky,
    Their legs have never encountered the fungi
And insects of the jungle, the monstrous forms and lives
    With which we have nothing, we like to hope, in common.
So, when one of them goes to the bad, the way his mind
                                                    works
    Remains comprehensible: to become a pimp
Or deal in fake jewellery or ruin a fine tenor voice
    For effects that bring down the house, could happen to all
But the best and the worst of us . . .

                                    That is why, I suppose,
    The best and worst never stayed here long but sought
Immoderate soils where the beauty was not so external,
    The light less public and the meaning of life
Something more than a mad camp. 'Come!' cried the granite
                                                    wastes,
    'How evasive is your humor, how accidental
Your kindest kiss, how permanent is death.' (Saints-to-be
    Slipped away sighing.) 'Come!' purred the clays and
                                                    gravels,
'On our plains there is room for armies to drill; rivers
    Wait to be tamed and slaves to construct you a tomb
In the grand manner: soft as the earth is mankind and both
    Need to be altered.' (Intendant Caesars rose and
Left, slamming the door.) But the really reckless were
                                                    fetched
    By an older colder voice, the oceanic whisper:
'I am the solitude that asks and promises nothing;
    That is how I shall set you free. There is no love;
There are only the various envies, all of them sad.'

    They were right, my dear, all those voices were right
And still are; this land is not the sweet home that it looks,
    Nor its peace the historical calm of a site

Where something was settled once and for all: A backward
   And dilapidated province, connected
To the big busy world by a tunnel, with a certain
   Seedy appeal, is that all it is now? Not quite:
It has a worldly duty which in spite of itself
   It does not neglect, but calls into question
All the Great Powers assume; it disturbs our rights. The poet,
   Admired for his earnest habit of calling
The sun the sun, his mind Puzzle, is made uneasy
   By these marble statues which so obviously doubt
His antimythological myth; and these gamins,
   Pursuing the scientist down the tiled colonnade
With such lively offers, rebuke his concern for Nature's
   Remotest aspects: I, too, am reproached, for what
And how much you know. Not to lose time, not to get
                                             caught,
   Not to be left behind, not, please! to resemble
The beasts who repeat themselves, or a thing like water
   Or stone whose conduct can be predicted, these
Are our Common Prayer, whose greatest comfort is music
   Which can be made anywhere, is invisible,
And does not smell. In so far as we have to look forward
   To death as a fact, no doubt we are right: But if
Sins can be forgiven, if bodies rise from the dead,
   These modifications of matter into
Innocent athletes and gesticulating fountains,
   Made solely for pleasure, make a further point:
The blessed will not care what angle they are regarded from,
   Having nothing to hide. Dear, I know nothing of
Either, but when I try to imagine a faultless love
   Or the life to come, what I hear is the murmur
Of underground streams, what I see is a limestone landscape.

Cattivo Tempo

Sirocco brings the minor devils:
A slamming of doors
At four in the morning
Announces they are back,
Grown insolent and fat
On cheesy literature
And corny dramas,
Nibbar, demon
Of ga-ga and bêtise,
Tubervillus, demon
Of gossip and spite.

Nibbar to the writing-room
Plausibly to whisper
The nearly fine,
The almost true;
Beware of him, poet,
Lest, reading over
Your shoulder, he find
What makes him glad,
The manner arch,
The meaning blurred,
The poem bad.

Tubervillus to the dining-room
Intently to listen,
Waiting his cue;
Beware of him, friends,
Lest the talk at his prompting
Take the wrong turning,
The unbated tongue
In mischief blurt
The half-home-truth,
The fun turn ugly,
The jokes hurt.

Do not underrate them; merely
To tear up the poem,
To shut the mouth
Will defeat neither:
To have got you alone
Self-confined to your bedroom
Manufacturing there
From lewdness or self-care
Some whining unmanaged
Imp of your own,
That too is their triumph.

The proper riposte is to bore them;
To scurry the dull pen
Through dull correspondence,
To wag the sharp tongue
In pigeon Italian,
Asking the socialist
Barber to guess
Or the monarchist fisherman to tell
When the wind will change,
Outwitting hell
With human obviousness.

Their Lonely Betters

As I listened from a beach-chair in the shade
To all the noises that my garden made,
It seemed to me only proper that words
Should be withheld from vegetables and birds.

A robin with no Christian name ran through
The Robin-Anthem which was all it knew,
And rustling flowers for some third party waited
To say which pairs, if any, should get mated.

Not one of them was capable of lying,
There was not one which knew that it was dying
Or could have with a rhythm or a rhyme
Assumed responsibility for time.

Let them leave language to their lonely betters
Who count some days and long for certain letters;
We, too, make noises when we laugh or weep:
Words are for those with promises to keep.

Fleet Visit

The sailors come ashore
Out of their hollow ships,
Mild-looking middle-class boys
Who read the comic strips;
One baseball game is more
To them than fifty Troys.

They look a bit lost, set down
In this unamerican place
Where natives pass with laws
And futures of their own;
They are not here because
But only just-in-case.

The whore and ne'er-do-well
Who pester them with junk
In their grubby ways at least
Are serving the Social Beast;
They neither make nor sell –
No wonder they get drunk.

But their ships on the vehement blue
Of this harbor actually gain
From having nothing to do;
Without a human will
To tell them whom to kill
Their structures are humane

And, far from looking lost,
Look as if they were meant
To be pure abstract design
By some master of pattern and line,
Certainly worth every cent
Of the billions they must have cost.

Lauds

Among the leaves the small birds sing;
The crow of the cock commands awaking:
In solitude, for company.

Bright shines the sun on creatures mortal;
Men of their neighbors become sensible:
In solitude, for company.

The crow of the cock commands awaking;
Already the mass-bell goes dong-ding:
In solitude, for company.

Men of their neighbors become sensible;
God bless the Realm, God bless the People:
In solitude, for company.

Already the mass-bell goes dong-ding;
The dripping mill-wheel is again turning:
In solitude, for company.

God bless the Realm, God bless the People;
God bless this green world temporal:
In solitude, for company.

The dripping mill-wheel is again turning;
Among the leaves the small birds sing:
In solitude, for company.

Streams

(for Elizabeth Drew)

Dear water, clear water, playful in all your streams,
as you dash or loiter through life who does not love
    to sit beside you, to hear you and see you,
    pure being, perfect in music and movement?

Air is boastful at times, earth slovenly, fire rude,
but you in your bearing are always immaculate,
    the most well-spoken of all the older
    servants in the household of Mrs Nature.

Nobody suspects you of mocking him, for you still
use the same vocables you were using the day
    before that unexpected row which
    downed every hod on half-finished Babel,

and still talk to yourself: nowhere are you disliked;
arching your torso, you dive from a basalt sill,
    canter across white chalk, slog forward
    through red marls, the aboriginal pilgrim,

at home in all sections, but for whom we should be
idolaters of a single rock, kept apart
    by our landscapes, excluding as alien
    the tales and diets of all other strata.

How could we love the absent one if you did not keep
coming from a distance, or quite directly assist,
    as when past Iseult's tower you floated
    the willow pash-notes of wanted Tristram?

And Homo Ludens, surely, is your child, who make
fun of our feuds by opposing identical banks
    and transferring the loam from Huppim
    to Muppim and back each time you crankle.

Growth cannot add to your song: as unchristened brooks
already you whisper to ants what, as Brahma's son,
    descending his titanic staircase
  into Assam, to Himalayan bears you thunder.

And not even man can spoil you: his company
coarsens roses and dogs but, should he herd you through a
                                                    sluice
    to toil at a turbine, or keep you
  leaping in gardens for his amusement,

innocent still is your outcry, water, and there
even, to his soiled heart raging at what it is,
    tells of a sort of world, quite other,
  altogether different from this one

with its envies and passports, a polis like that
to which, in the name of scholars everywhere,
    Gaston Paris pledged his allegiance
  as Bismarck's siege-guns came within earshot.

Lately, in that dale of all Yorkshire's the loveliest,
where, off its fell-side helter-skelter, Kisdon Beck
    jumps into Swale with a boyish shouting,
  sprawled out on grass, I dozed for a second,

and found myself following a croquet tournament
in a calm enclosure, with thrushes popular:
    of all the players in that cool valley
  the best with the mallet was my darling.

While, on the wolds that begirdled it, wild old men
hunted with spades and hammers, monomaniac each,
    for a megalith or a fossil,
  and bird-watchers crept through mossy beech-woods.

Suddenly, over the lawn we started to run
for, lo, through the trees, in a cream and golden coach

       drawn by two baby locomotives,
      the god of mortal doting approached us,

flanked by his bodyguard, those hairy armigers in green
who laugh at thunderstorms and weep at a blue sky:
      He thanked us for our cheers of homage,
      and promised X and Y a passion undying.

With a wave of his torch he commanded a dance;
so round in a ring we flew, my dear on my right,
      when I awoke. But fortunate seemed that
      day because of my dream and enlightened,

and dearer, water, than ever your voice, as if
glad – though goodness knows why – to run with the human
                             race,

      wishing, I thought, the least of men their
      figures of splendor, their holy places.

A Permanent Way

Self-drivers may curse their luck,
Stuck on new-fangled trails,
But the good old train will jog
To the dogma of its rails,

And steam so straight ahead
That I cannot be led astray
By tempting scenes which occur
Along any permanent way.

Intriguing dales escape
Into hills of the shape I like,
Though, were I actually put
Where a foot-path leaves the pike

For some steep romantic spot,
I should ask what chance there is
Of at least a ten-dollar cheque
Or a family peck of a kiss:

But, forcibly held to my tracks,
I can safely relax and dream
Of a love and a livelihood
To fit that wood or stream;

And what could be greater fun,
Once one has chosen and paid,
Than the inexpensive delight
Of a choice one might have made?

The Old Man's Road

Across the Great Schism, through our whole landscape,
Ignoring God's Vicar and God's Ape,

Under their noses, unsuspected,
The Old Man's Road runs as it did

When a light subsoil, a simple ore
Were still in vogue: true to His wherefore,

By stiles, gates, hedge-gaps it goes
Over ploughland, woodland, cow meadows,

Past shrines to a cosmological myth
No heretic today would be caught dead with,

Near hill-top rings that were so safe then,
Now stormed easily by small children

(Shepherds use bits in the high mountains,
Hamlets take stretches for Lovers' Lanes),

Then through cities threads its odd way,
Now without gutters, a Thieves' Alley,

Now with green lamp-posts and white curb,
The smart Crescent of a high-toned suburb,

Giving wide berth to an old Cathedral,
Running smack through a new Town Hall,

Unlookable for, by logic, by guess:
Yet some strike it, and are struck fearless.

No life can know it, but no life
That sticks to this course can be made captive,

And who wander with it are not stopped at
Borders by guards of some Theocrat,

Crossing the pass so almost where
His searchlight squints but no closer

(And no further where it might by chance):
So in summer sometimes, without hindrance,

Apotropaically scowling, a tinker
Shuffles past, in the waning year

Potters a coleopterist, poking
Through yellow leaves, and a youth in spring

Trots by after a new excitement,
His true self, hot on the scent.

The Old Man leaves his Road to those
Who love it no less since it lost purpose,

Who never ask what History is up to,
So cannot act as if they knew:

Assuming a freedom its Powers deny,
Denying its Powers, they pass freely.

There Will Be No Peace

    Though mild clear weather
Smile again on the shire of your esteem
And its colors come back, the storm has changed you:
    You will not forget, ever,
The darkness blotting out hope, the gale
    Prophesying your downfall.

    You must live with your knowledge.
Way back, beyond, outside of you are others,
In moonless absences you never heard of,
    Who have certainly heard of you,
Beings of unknown number and gender:
    And they do not like you.

    What have you done to them?
Nothing? Nothing is not an answer:
You will come to believe – how can you help it? –
    That you did, you did do something;
You will find yourself wishing you could make them laugh,
    You will long for their friendship.

    There will be no peace.
Fight back, then, with such courage as you have
And every unchivalrous dodge you know of,
    Clear in your conscience on this:
Their cause, if they had one, is nothing to them now;
    They hate for hate's sake.

Limbo Culture

The tribes of Limbo, travellers report,
On first encounter seem much like ourselves;
They keep their houses practically clean,
Their watches round about a standard time,
They serve you almost appetising meals:
But no one says he saw a Limbo child.

The language spoken by the tribes of Limbo
Has many words far subtler than our own
To indicate how much, how little, something
Is pretty closely or not quite the case,
But none you could translate by *Yes* or *No*,
Nor do its pronouns distinguish between Persons.

In tales related by the tribes of Limbo,
Dragon and Knight set to with fang and sword
But miss their rival always by a hair's-breadth,
Old Crone and Stripling pass a crucial point,
She seconds early and He seconds late,
A magic purse mistakes the legal tender:

'And so,' runs their concluding formula,
'Prince and Princess are nearly married still.'
Why this concern, so marked in Limbo culture,
This love for inexactness? Could it be
A Limbo tribesman only loves himself?
For that, we know, cannot be done exactly.

Walks

I choose the road from here to there
When I've a scandalous tale to bear,
Tools to return or books to lend
To someone at the other end.

Returning afterwards, although
I meet my footsteps toe to toe,
The road looks altogether new
Now that is done I meant to do.

But I avoid it when I take
A walker's walk for walking's sake:
The repetition it involves
Raises a doubt it never solves.

What good or evil angel bid
Me stop exactly when I did?
What would have happened had I gone
A kilometre further on?

No, when a fidget in the soul
Or cumulus clouds invite a stroll,
The route I pick goes roundabout
To finish where it started out.

It gets me home, this curving track,
Without my having to turn back,
Nor does it leave it up to me
To say how long my walk shall be,

Yet satisfies a moral need
By turning behavior into deed,
For I have boxed the compass when
I enter my front door again.

The heart, afraid to leave her shell,
Demands a hundred yards as well
Between my personal abode
And either sort of public road,

Making, when it is added too,
The straight a T, the round a Q,
Allowing me in rain or shine
To call both walks entirely mine,

A lane no traveller would use,
Where prints that do not fit my shoes
Have looked for me and, like enough,
Were made by someone whom I love.

Dame Kind

Steatopygous, sow-dugged
                    and owl-headed,
To Whom – Whom else? – the first innocent blood
                    was formally shed
By a chinned mammal that hard times
                    had turned carnivore,
From Whom his first promiscuous orgy
                    begged a downpour
To speed the body-building cereals
                    of a warmer age:
Now who put *us*, we should like to know,
                    in *Her* manage?

Strait-laced She never was
                    and has not grown more so
Since the skeptical academies got wind
                    of the *Chi-Rho*
St Cuckoo's wooden church for Her
                    where on Green Sundays
Bald hermits celebrate a wordless
                    cult in Her praise:
So pocket your fifty sonnets, Bud;
                    tell Her a myth
Of unpunishable gods and all the girls
                    they interfered with.

Haven't we spotted Her Picked Winners
                    whom She cossets, ramparts
And does the handsome by? Didn't the darlings
                    have cold hearts?
. . . ONE BOMB WOULD BE ENOUGH . . . Now look
                    who's thinking gruesome!
Brother, you're worse than a lonesome Peeper
                    or a He-Virgin

Who nightly abhors the Primal Scene
                    in medical Latin:
She mayn't be all She might be but
                    She *is* our Mum.

You can't tell *us* your hypochondriac
                    Blue-Stocking from Provence
Who makes the clock-work arcadies go round
                    is worth twopence;
You won't find a steady in *that* museum
                    unless you prefer
Tea with a shapeless angel to bedtime
                    with a lovely monster:
Before you catch it for your mim look
                    and gnostic chirrup,
Ask the Kind Lady who fitted you out
                    to fix you up.

Supposing even (through misdirections
                    or your own mischief)
You do land in that anomalous duchy,
                    Her remotest fief,
Where four eyes encounter in two
                    one mirror perilous
As the clear rock-basin that stultified
                    frigid Narcissus,
Where tongues stammer on a First Name,
                    bereft of guile,
And common snub-nosed creatures are abashed
                    at a face in profile,

Even there, as your blushes invoke its Guardian
                    (whose true invocable
Name is singular for each true heart
                    and false to tell)
To sacre your courtship ritual so
                    it deserve a music

More solemn than the he-hawing
                    of a salesman's limerick,
Do a bow to the Coarse Old Party that wrought you
                    an alderliefest
Of the same verbose and sentient kidney,
                    grateful not least

For all the dirty work She did.
                    How many hundreds
Of lawful, unlawful, both equally
                    loveless beds,
Of lying endearments, crooked questions,
                    crookeder answers,
Of bawling matches, sarcastic silences,
                    megrims, tears,
How much half-witted horse-play and sheer
                    bloody misrule
It took to bring you two together
                    both on schedule?

You

Really, must you,
Over-familiar
Dense companion,
Be there always?
The bond between us
Is chimerical surely:
Yet I cannot break it.

Must I, born for
Sacred play,
Turn base mechanic
So you may worship
Your secular bread,
With no thought
Of the value of time?

Thus far I have known your
Character only
From its pleasanter side,
But you know I know
A day will come
When you grow savage
And hurt me badly.

Totally stupid?
Would that you were:
But, no, you plague me
With tastes I was fool enough
Once to believe in.
Bah!, blockhead:
I know where you learned them.

Can I trust you even
On creaturely fact?
I suspect strongly

You hold some dogma
Of positive truth,
And feed me fictions:
I shall never prove it.

Oh, I know how you came by
A sinner's cranium,
How between two glaciers
The master-chronometer
Of an innocent primate
Altered its tempi:
That explains nothing.

Who tinkered and why?
Why am I certain,
Whatever your faults are,
The fault is mine,
Why is loneliness not
A chemical discomfort,
Nor Being a smell?

A Change of Air

Corns, heartburn, sinus headaches, such minor ailments
Tell of estrangement between your name and you,
Advise a change of air: heed them, but let
The modesty of their discomfort warn you
Against the flashy errands of your dreams.

To grow a sailor's beard, don monkish garb,
Or trade in an agglutinative tongue
With a stone-age culture, would be molly-coddling:
To go Elsewhere is to withdraw from movement;
A side-step, a short one, will convey you thither.

Although its chaffinches, maybe, have learned
The dialect of another river-basin,
A fault transformed the local building stone,
It has a priest, a post-mistress, an usher,
Its children know they are not to beg from strangers.

Within its average elsewhereishness
Your name is as a mirror answers, yourself
How you behave in shops, the tips you give:
It sides with neither, being outside both,
But welcomes both with healing disregard.

Nor, when you both return here (for you will)
Where luck and instinct originally brought you,
Will it salute your reconciliation
With farewell rites, or populate your absence
With reverent and irreverent anecdote.

No study of your public re-appearance
Will show, as judgement on a cure demands,
A sudden change in love, ideas, or diet:
Your sojourn Elsewhere will remain a wordless
Hiatus in your voluble biography.

Fanatic scholarship at most may prove
That you resigned from some Committee, unearth
A letter from the Grand-Duke to his cousin,
Remarking, among more important gossip,
That you seem less amusing than you were.

The Birth of Architecture
(for John Bayley)

From gallery-grave and the hunt of a wren-king
    to Low Mass and trailer-camp
is hardly a tick by the carbon-clock, but I
    don't count that way nor do you:
already it is millions of heart-beats ago
    back to the Bicycle Age,
before which is no *After* for me to measure,
    just a still prehistoric *Once*
where anything could happen. To you, to me,
    Stonehenge and Chartres Cathedral,
the Acropolis, Blenheim, the Albert Memorial
    are works by the same Old Man
under different names: we know what He did,
    what, even, He thought He thought,
but we don't see why. (To get that, one would have
    to be selfish in His way,
without concrete or grapefruit.) It's our turn now
    to puzzle the unborn. No world
wears as well as it should but, mortal or not,
    a world has still to be built
because of what we can see from our windows,
    that Immortal Commonwealth
which is there regardless: it's in perfect taste
    and it's never boring but
it won't quite do. Among its populations
    are masons and carpenters
who build the most exquisite shelters and safes,
    but no architects, any more
than there are heretics or bounders: to take
    umbrage at death, to construct
a second nature of tomb and temple, lives
    must know the meaning of *If.*

POSTSCRIPT

Some thirty inches from my nose
The frontier of my Person goes,
And all the untilled air between
Is private *pagus* or demesne.
Stranger, unless with bedroom eyes
I beckon you to fraternise,
Beware of rudely crossing it:
I have no gun, but I can spit.

Recitative by Death

Ladies and gentlemen, you have made most remarkable
    Progress, and progress, I agree, is a boon;
You have built more automobiles than are parkable,
    Crashed the sound-barrier, and may very soon
    Be setting up juke-boxes on the Moon:
But I beg to remind you that, despite all that,
I, Death, still am and will always be Cosmocrat.

Still I sport with the young and daring; at my whim,
    The climber steps upon the rotten boulder,
The undertow catches boys as they swim,
    The speeder steers onto the slippery shoulder:
    With others I wait until they are older
Before assigning, according to my humor,
To one a coronary, to one a tumor.

Liberal my views upon religion and race;
    Tax-posture, credit-rating, social ambition
Cut no ice with me. We shall meet face to face,
    Despite the drugs and lies of your physician,
    The costly euphemisms of the mortician:
Westchester matron and Bowery bum,
Both shall dance with me when I rattle my drum.

Et in Arcadia Ego

Who, now, seeing Her so
Happily married,
Housewife, helpmate to Man,

Can imagine the screeching
Virago, the Amazon,
Earth-Mother was?

Her jungle-growths
Are abated, Her exorbitant
Monsters abashed,

Her soil mumbled,
Where crops, aligned precisely,
Will soon be orient:

Levant or couchant,
Well-daunted thoroughbreds
Graze on mead and pasture,

A church-clock sub-divides the day,
Up the lane at sundown
Geese podge home.

As for Him:
What has happened to the Brute
Epics and nightmares tell of?

No bishops pursue
Their archdeacons with axes,
In the crumbling lair

Of a robber baron
Sightseers picnic
Who carry no daggers.

I well might think myself
A humanist
Could I manage not to see

How the autobahn
Thwarts the landscape
In godless Roman arrogance,

The farmer's children
Tip-toe past the shed
Where the gelding-knife is kept.

Since

On a mid-December day,
frying sausages
for myself, I abruptly
felt under fingers
thirty years younger the rim
of a steering-wheel,
on my cheek the parching wind
of an August noon,
as passenger beside me
You as then you were.

Slap across a veg-growing
alluvial plain
we raced in clouds of white dust,
and geese fled screaming
as we missed them by inches,
making a bee-line
for mountains gradually
enlarging eastward,
joyfully certain nightfall
would occasion joy.

It did. In a flagged kitchen
we were served broiled trout
and a rank cheese: for a while
we talked by the fire,
then, carrying candles, climbed
steep stairs. Love was made
then and there: so halcyoned,
soon we fell asleep
to the sound of a river
swabbling through a gorge.

Since then, other enchantments
have blazed and faded,
enemies changed their address,
and War made ugly
an uncountable number
of unknown neighbors,
precious as us to themselves:
but round your image
there is no fog, and the Earth
can still astonish.

Of what, then, should I complain,
pottering about
a neat suburban kitchen?
Solitude? Rubbish!
It's social enough with real
faces and landscapes
for whose friendly countenance
I at least can learn
to live with obesity
and a little fame.

River Profile

Our body is a moulded river – NOVALIS

Out of a bellicose fore-time, thundering
head-on collisions of cloud and rock in an
up-thrust, crevasse-and-avalanche, troll country,
deadly to breathers,

it whelms into our picture below the melt-line,
where tarns lie frore under frowning cirques, goat-bell,
wind-breaker, fishing-rod, miner's-lamp country,
already at ease with

the mien and gestures that become its kindness,
in streams, still anonymous, still jumpable,
flows as it should through any declining country
in probing spirals.

Soon of a size to be named and the cause of
dirty in-fighting among rival agencies,
down a steep stair, penstock-and-turbine country,
it plunges ram-stam,

to foam through a wriggling gorge incised in softer
strata, hemmed between crags that nauntle heaven,
robber-baron, tow-rope, portage-way country,
nightmare of merchants.

Disemboguing from foothills, now in hushed meanders,
now in riffling braids, it vaunts across a senile
plain, well-entered, chateau-and-cider-press country,
its regal progress

gallanted for a while by quibbling poplars,
then by chimneys: led off to cool and launder
retort, steam-hammer, gasometer country,
it changes color.

Polluted, bridged by girders, banked by concrete,
now it bisects a polyglot metropolis,
ticker-tape, taxi, brothel, foot-lights country,
à-la-mode always.

Broadening or burrowing to the moon's phases,
turbid with pulverised wastemantle, on through
flatter, duller, hotter, cotton-gin country
it scours, approaching

the tidal mark where it puts off majesty,
disintegrates, and through swamps of a delta,
punting-pole, fowling-piece, oyster-tongs country,
wearies to its final

act of surrender, effacement, atonement
in a huge amorphous aggregate no cuddled
attractive child ever dreams of, non-country,
image of death as

a spherical drew-drop of life. Unlovely
monsters, our tales believe, can be translated
too, even as water, the selfless mother
of all especials.

A Mosaic for Marianne Moore

(on the occasion of her eightieth birthday, November 15th, 1967)

The concluded gardens of personal liking
are enchanted habitats
where real toads may catch imaginary flies
and the climate will accommodate the tiger
and the polar-bear.

So in the middle of yours (where it is human
to sit) we see you sitting
in a wide-brimmed hat beneath a monkey-puzzle,
at your feet the beasts you animated for us
by thinking of them.

Your lion with ferocious chrysanthemum head,
your jerboa, erect on
his Chippendale claw, your pelican behaving
like charred paper, your musk-ox who smells of water,
your fond nautilus,

cope with what surprises them and greet the stranger
in a mid-western accent,
even that bum, the unelephantine creature
who is certainly here to worship and often
selected to mourn.

Egocentric, eccentric, he will name a cat
Peter, a new car *Edsel*,
emphasise his own birthday and a few others
he thinks deserve it, as to-day we stress your name,
Miss Marianne Moore

who, fastidious but fair, are unaffronted
by those whose disposition
it is to affront, who beg the cobra's pardon,
are always on time and never would yourself write
error with four *r*'s.

For poems, dolphin-graceful as carts from Sweden,
our thank-you should be a right
good salvo of barks: it's much too muffled to say
'how well and with what unfreckled integrity
it has all been done.'

August 1968

The Ogre does what ogres can,
Deeds quite impossible for Man,
But one prize is beyond his reach,
The Ogre cannot master Speech.
About a subjugated plain,
Among its desperate and slain,
The Ogre stalks with hands on hips,
While drivel gushes from his lips.

Pseudo-Questions

Who could possibly approve of Metternich
and his Thought Police? Yet in a liberal
milieu would Adalbert Stifter have written
    his noble idylls?

Vice-versa, what God-fearing Magistrate
would dream of shaking hands with a financial
crook and Anti-Semite? Yet Richard Wagner
    wrought masterpieces.

Wild horses could not drag me to debates on
Art and Society: critics with credos,
Christian or Marxist, should keep their trap shut,
    lest they spout nonsense.

The Aliens

(*for William Gray*)

Wide though the interrupt be that divides us, runers and
counters,
from the Old World of the Plants, all lapped in a tolerant
silence,
where, by the grace of chlorophyll, few of them ever have
taken
life and not one put a sceptical question, we nod them as
neighbours
who, to conclude from their friendly response to a gardener's
handling,
like to be given the chance to get more than a self-education.
As for the hot-blooded Beasts, we didn't need Darwin to tell
us
horses and rabbits and mice are our cognates, the double-
voiced song-birds
cousins, however removed: unique as we seem, we, too, are
shovelled out into the cold, poodle-naked, as male or as
female,
grab at and gobble up proteins, drop dung, perform the
ungainly
brute-with-two-backs until, dared and doddered by age, we
surrender,
lapse into stagnant stuff, while they by retaining a constant
visible shape through a lifetime, accord with our human idea
of
having a Self. They also, we cannot but fancy, are peering
at a horizon as we do, aware of, however obscurely,
more than they must be concerned with, and vaguely elated
at being
someone who's up and about: yes, even their humblest have,
surely,
nosed a few steps on the hazardous foreright to courage,

utterance, joy and collateral love. That is why, in our folk-
                                                          tales,
toads and squirrels can talk, in our epics the great be
                                                 compared to
lions or foxes or eagles.
                         But between us and the Insects,
namely nine-tenths of the living, there grins a prohibitive
                                                       fracture
empathy cannot transgress: (What Saint made a friend of a
                                                    roach or
preached to an ant-hill?) Unrosed by a shame, unendorsed
                                                    by a sorrow,
blank to a fear of failure, they daunt alike the believer's
faith in a fatherly providence and the atheist's dogma of
                                                       purely
random events. To begin as a crawling insatiable eater,
then to be buried and mortify, then to emerge from the cere-
                                                          cloth
winged and mateable, brilliantly coloured, a sipper of juices,
yet a compulsive hunter and hoarder, must do havoc to any
unitive sense. To insert them, excuse those unamiable towns
                                                        where
sex is reserved for the Few and the many animate tool-kits
perish from overwear, one is tempted to cook up a Gnostic
myth of an earlier Fall, preceding by aeons the Reptiles:
Adam, a crab-like creature who'd just wriggled out of a
                                                       steamy
ocean where he had failed at making a living and now lay
moribund, choked, on a shore without song. Unto whom the
                                                       Seducer,
not our romantic Satan but a clever cartesian Archon,
coaxingly thus: *Not doing very well, are you, poor deathling,
no, and unlikely to do any better, thanks to the schemes of
We-Know-Whom. (He's a Precious but logic was never His
                                                         forte.)*
Freedom may manage in Heaven with Incorporeals, but for

ghosted extended matter the consequence is to be doomed to
err where an error is mortal. But trust me and live, for I do
                                                    know
clearly what needs to be done. If I programme your ganglia for
                                                    you,
you shall inherit the earth.

                              Such a myth, we all know, is no
                                                    answer.
What they mean to themselves or to God is a meaningless
                                                    question:
they to us are quite simply what we must never become.

Short Ode to the Cuckoo

No one now imagines you answer idle questions
– *How long shall I live? How long remain single?*
Will butter be cheaper? – nor does your shout make
    husbands uneasy.

Compared with arias by the great performers
such as the merle, your two-note act is kid-stuff:
our most hardened crooks are sincerely shocked by
    your nesting habits.

Science, Aesthetics, Ethics, may huff and puff but they
cannot extinguish your magic: you marvel
the commuter as you wondered the savage.
    Hence, in my diary,

where I normally enter nothing but social
engagements and, lately, the death of friends, I
scribble year after year when I first hear you,
    of a holy moment.

Aubade

(In Memoriam Eugen Rosenstock-Huessy)

Beckoned anew to a World
where wishes alter nothing,
expelled from the padded cell
of Sleep and re-admitted
to involved Humanity,
again, as wrote Augustine,
I know that I am and will,
I am willing and knowing,
I will to be and to know,
facing in four directions,
outwards and inwards in Space,
observing and reflecting,
backwards and forwards through Time,
recalling and forecasting.

Out there, to the Heart, there are
no dehumanised Objects,
each one has its Proper Name,
there is no Neuter Gender:
Flowers fame their splendid shades,
Trees are proud of their posture,
Stones are delighted to lie
just where they are. Few bodies
comprehend, though, an order,
few can obey or rebel,
so, when they must be managed,
Love is no help: We must opt
to eye them as mere Others,
must count, weigh, measure, compel.

Within a Place, not of Names
but of Personal Pronouns,
where I hold council with Me

and recognise as present
Thou and Thou comprising We,
unmindful of the meinie,
all those We think of as They.
No voice is raised in quarrel,
but quietly We converse,
by turns relate tall stories,
at times just sit in silence,
and on fit occasion I
sing verses *sotto-voce*,
made on behalf of Us all.

But Time, the domain of Deeds,
calls for a complex Grammar
with many Moods and Tenses,
and prime the Imperative.
We are free to choose our paths
but choose We must, no matter
where they lead, and the tales We
tell of the Past must be true.
Human Time is a City
where each inhabitant has
a political duty
nobody else can perform,
made cogent by Her Motto:
Listen, Mortals, Lest Ye Die.

Address to the Beasts

For us who, from the moment
we first are worlded,
lapse into disarray,

who seldom know exactly
what we are up to,
and, as a rule, don't want to,

what a joy to know,
even when we can't see or hear you,
that you are around,

though very few of you
find us worth looking at,
unless we come too close.

To you all scents are sacred
except our smell and those
we manufacture.

How promptly and ably
you execute Nature's policies,
and are never

lured into misconduct
except by some unlucky
chance imprinting.

Endowed from birth with good manners,
you wag no snobbish elbows,
don't leer,

don't look down your nostrils,
nor poke them into another
creature's business.

Your own habitations
are cosy and private, not
pretentious temples.

Of course, you have to take lives
to keep your own, but never
kill for applause.

Compared with even your greediest,
how Non-U
our hunting gentry seem.

Exempt from taxation,
you have never felt the need
to become literate,

but your oral cultures
have inspired our poets to pen
dulcet verses,

and, though unconscious of God
your Sung Eucharists are
more hallowed than ours.

Instinct is commonly said
to rule you: I would call it
Common Sense.

If you cannot engender
a genius like Mozart,
neither can you

plague the earth
with brilliant sillies like Hegel
or clever nasties like Hobbes.

Shall we ever become adulted,
as you all soon do?
It seems unlikely.

Indeed, one balmy day,
we might well become
not fossils, but vapour.

Distinct now,
in the end we shall join you
(how soon all corpses look alike),

but you exhibit no signs
of knowing that you are sentenced.
Now, could that be why

we upstarts are often
jealous of your innocence,
but never envious?

No, Plato, No

I can't imagine anything
    that I would less like to be
than a disincarnate Spirit,
    unable to chew or sip
or make contact with surfaces
    or breathe the scents of summer
or comprehend speech and music
    or gaze at what lies beyond.
No, God has placed me exactly
    where I'd have chosen to be:
the sub-lunar world is such fun,
    where Man is male or female
and gives Proper Names to all things.

    I can, however, conceive
that the organs Nature gave Me,
    my ductless glands, for instance,
slaving twenty-four hours a day
    with no show of resentment
to gratify Me, their Master,
    and keep Me in decent shape,
(not that I give them their orders,
    I wouldn't know what to yell),
dream of another existence
    than that they have known so far:
yes, it well could be that my Flesh
    is praying for 'Him' to die,
so setting Her free to become
    irresponsible Matter.